THREADS

FUTUREPOEM BOOKS
NEW YORK CITY
2007

THREADS

JILL MAGI

FIRST EDITION | FIRST PRINTING

This edition first published in paperback by Futurepoem books
www.futurepoem.com
Editor: Dan Machlin
Guest Editors: Ammiel Alcalay, Jen Hofer, Prageeta Sharma

Design: Anthony Monahan (am@anthonymonahan.com)

Cover & all interior images © Jill Magi

Typesetting: Garrett Kalleberg
Copyediting: Marcella Durand

Cover and text set in Scala.
Printed in the United States of America on acid-free paper.

This project is supported by an award from the National Endowment for the Arts, and by grants from the New York State Council on the Arts, the New York Community Trust, and the Fund for Poetry. Futurepoem books receives nonprofit sponsorship for grants and donations through Fractured Atlas Productions, Inc., a 501(c)3 tax exempt organization. Contributions are fully tax-deductible and much needed!

Distributed to the trade by Small Press Distribution, Berkeley, California
Toll-free number (U.S. only): 800.869.7553
Bay area/International: 510.524.1668
orders@spdbooks.org
www.spdbooks.org

I wish to express gratitude to Futurepoem books editor Dan Machlin, as well as guest editors Ammiel Alcalay, Jen Hofer, and Prageeta Sharma. Thanks to Ammiel Alcalay and Jen Hofer for their generous editorial guidance. Thanks to Doug Dunbebin for his invaluable role, beyond technical skill, in realizing the images in this book. Alicia Askenase provided editorial insights at a crucial stage, and to her I am very grateful. Thanks to Jonny Farrow, Trina Magi, and Johannah Rodgers for reading numerous versions of this book over the years. Thanks also to Darcy DiIorio for encouraging my visual work. I am grateful for the support from my friends and colleagues John Calagione, Debbie Edwards-Anderson, and Warren Orange at The City College Center for Worker Education. Thanks to John Calagione for pointing me toward *Seeing Like a State: How Certain Schemes to Improve the Human Condition Have Failed* by James C. Scott and *Imagined Communities: Reflections on the Origin and Spread of Nationalism* by Benedict Anderson, two books that helped shape my approach to the subject matter. I thank those who have been my teachers, encouraging me in all stages of this project: Michael Willard, Mark Mirsky, Leopoldo Fuentes, Laura Hinton, Juliana Spahr, Renee Gladman, Cecilia Vicuña, and Jordan Davis. To my students, who have so freely shared their love of language and courage to learn, I am grateful. Finally, for providing documents and stories and the sounds of "eesti keel," I owe a debt of gratitude to Tarmu Magi, Eino Magi, Liisa and Eduard Magi, and my entire family.

Portions of this book have been published, in somewhat different forms, in *The Brooklyn Rail*, *HOW2*, *Aufgabe*, *Chain*, *Pierogi Press*, and *Raised in a Barn*. Thanks to those editors for their support.

for Jonny

It is a sovereign nation as the sky is large. I write in the haze of alleged safety, June being never-night.

The attachment of cell phones to the belt and new umbrellas over empty café tables is read as progress. Billboards are few and feature Estonian beer. Here, a blond man without a shirt sweats for the company owned by Swedes. Wet glass appeal, his capitalism reaches toward a nation of leaning, of platform shoes on cobblestones, drunk on miniskirts.

Museum labels peel away from the wall and I strain to see as some lightbulbs are out, my perspective growing dim.

Watchdogs bark back Russian neighbors or the perhaps gypsies, having intermarried.

Excavations topped with weeds in bloom, barrels of garbage burn inappropriately. Precarious scaffolding wraps up bullet holes and dredging the lake is necessary while I expected something closer to Europe, tourism, or at least not that smell.

My money belt is moist against my skin as I watch electrical wires in the wind, slapping against cement apartment buildings without front doors.

I hand her unfamiliar money. She unfolds,

"Here is map" drawing a circle

"Here you are now."

I agree, appearing to be free of questions though it is not clear in which

direction I will go next.

Between "you" and "are" her tongue struggles.

I understand. "Thank you."

Amber return, once fluid, hardened breath-trap.

Sap turns to stone as these sounds conjure whose memories?

Air pocket scarred with debris, a dictionary. His voice on tape translates

my flat speech:

too few vowels and endings that stop, closed in by consonants.

Flash card fossils. How to count, the days, the months,

I am a student, where is the bathroom, the night is long,

over the threshold, write me a letter.

Anton pani põllutöölehe heinamaa-... õue.

Estonia has no internal administrative ...

0 — 50 Kilometers
0 — 50 Miles

Lambert — Conic Projection, SP

Baltic Sea — SAILED TO SWEDEN APRIL 1944

Vormsi

Kärdla
Hiiumaa — Haapsa[lu]

NARROW GAUGE (IN 1944)

Rapla

Lelle

...ldiski — Tallinn — NÕM[ME]
KEILA — SAUE

...id ja käsivarred läbi õreda õlule visa-
...d rohelise rüü valendasid.

Midagi oli ta näinud, ilusat, veetlevat, ja unistusse tõmbavat, aga see oli kui ...ilvesagar õhuks auranud ja jä- ...ainult läbipaistmatu põh-

Tema puik... vale iseenesesse, nagu kalamehe õng jõe põhja kõntsa, kannu külge või sõga suhu.

Unistades hulkus ta tänavat mööda alla kaasiku poole ja läks oma lapse-põlve seltsiliste, sirgete valgejalgsete neit-site keskele kõndima, kelle jumedad rin...

6

...as nähtud ...nine viirastus ja nüüd võis ta vaadelda ...eda kujustunud unistuspilti, ja mäleatu- ...sest teadvusega täiendavaid joon tõm- mata.

See oli Tülba Tõnise uhke tütar Truuta, kellega ta siit üheskoos sajad korrad koolist koju poole tulnud. Assa Kustas

7

Fingers blister against pages of refugees or dead or missing

as words are the only clues we have and the space between

                        —the epistemology of touch demanding attention

to presence and absence both

underlight on a seagull's wings

            a sudden change in flight path.

Dear refugee: plane is faster than boat.

Looking is the finding, leaving arrives.

My push to the right of the page toward history.

The gull perches.

The eyes must be large enough to take the thread freely.

Thread, tape, and cord: durable and used for strengthening and hinging the sections.

A torn leaf is repaired by marrying the overlapping edges and print together with a needle. Position it under the missing part. Some loss is inevitable.

The grain of the original is ascertained.

Needing more time to arrive, I sit on a bench between ferry terminal and city gate, imagining that my father's history is visible on my face. An uncertain expression. Perhaps sadness or certain Estonian features such as hair color or the eyes, though in any other context, I do not believe in this.

They watch. I open the ziplock bag that holds my notebook, still in the right place, protected.

THE STORY OF ELDER EDUARD MAGI

Eduard Magi was born September 6, 1897 in Tartu, (D___at) Estonia, a small country by the Baltic Sea across from Finland. Father, Hendri___gi, a gardener, Mother, Kadri Joosep. Education: Public school and self-educa___n, plus SDA seminaries in Newbold, England and Takoma Park, Maryland. The tuitio___or public school was earned by painting houses, because his mother became a ___ow in her young age with three children. Faith: Lutheran. Conferred and marrie___ in the Lutheran church. Married to Liisa Bloom on May 20, 1918. She was born ___mber 5, 1896 in Viljandi, Estonia. Their children: Eino Magi, M.D., born March 3___1919 in Tartu, Estonia. Presently living in Silver Spring, Maryland. Kaljo Mag___Ph.D., born November 22, 1922, Tartu, Estonia. Died July 22, 1976 in Riverside___California. Tarmu Magi, born February 25, 1932, Tartu, Estonia, presently in ___amuchy, New Jersey.

The good mother of his wife, Ann Bloom was a fai___ful SDA member. She prayed in her church that the Lord would help her to win at ___east one of her seven children to the Adventist church. Her prayers were answered ___many fold. Before she died there were three of her daughters, two sons-in-law ___d two sisters of one of them in the SDA church. The conversion of Eduwrd and L___a opened the way of relatives to accept the Advent message. Eduard and Liisa M___were baptized together with 27 other young persons by Elder Johan Sprohge or ___June 26, 1919 in Tartu, in the river "Emajogi" (Mothers-river).

As their baptism had opened the way f___the relatives to come to the SDA church, in later years there has been baptized t___r children, grandchildren and other relatives. God answered the prayers o___true adventist mother sevenfold by seven-fold. . .

Coming to the church, Eduard be___an to sell and to distribute Adventist literature and soon the Estonian Conferen___ppointed him as editor for a new magazine, "The Friend of the Youth". He bec___e also a volunteer or substitute speaker in his home church in Tartu and in ___l Eduard became a Bibleworkers of the Estonian Conference and was later ordai___d on June 23, 1928.

(next page)

Inside, I follow the network of roads pressing toward the center, a concluding city square where languages mix and trade. I read cracks in the city walls, cobblestones pulled up. Grass, time, and water push edges apart under my feet and buildings whisper against my shoulders.

I DOUBT THE ACCURACY OF THIS MAP

on the margin, my father's handwriting

(They say that) this window had to be closed. (They say that) gardens had to be grown. (They say that) life has been completely rearranged to the Soviet pattern. (They say that) this page was torn and The Estonian Book is not very old.

Mitte nüüd, unusta nälja järin
ma olen väsinud, Jumal.

5.) Kui tuleb vastus, nu xi
kui müürsx plahva
sähvatab, siis   mbatab,
st varsti' ala   ab ja valgus
ma olen   een selgerti
6.) Se   a surnud. Prand
väsinud.

polnud elu, mis mina
pääautkesin. Ma ei mädnud
Vitnami. Aga kui peaos määlma
le tulema näku
Minu elu ei antud, aga mitte
asjata. Ma olen väsinud
Samal, ag nitte ja tulen
koji

4) palm üks teine päevan autäis
võitlust ja ta plust

Say: Sinul on isa. You have a father. Temal on tool. She has a chair. It is just as it sounds. Mul on sõber. I have a friend. Öö on pikk. The night is long.

The sound of an owl or the wind. Kirjutama mulle üks kiri. Write me a letter. Try these sounds. Uks avati. The door was opened. You have a father. We read. Try. Say it. I have a book. How to write this book.

To the dinner table I brought Angela Davis to which he said, "Why don't you live there and see if you like it."

Our various maxims so saturated by the sea that few words stand up against—

a lapel pin atop polyester, of the Estonian flag (illegal there) here flying along with the American, enameled. His inside pocket full of the question, "Do you know Estonia?" He brings pamphlets about The Annexation for the waitress, everywhere.

The American industrial farm will not be called collectivized and the Soviets meet secretly with agricultural engineers in Montana, sharing a crop of modernist faith.

Engineer precedes father precedes master precedes oneself, even independence. Reading down the column: isa, isegi, iseseis.

A peasant with a bit of land was a one-foot. Johnny Workman was the ideal American boy.

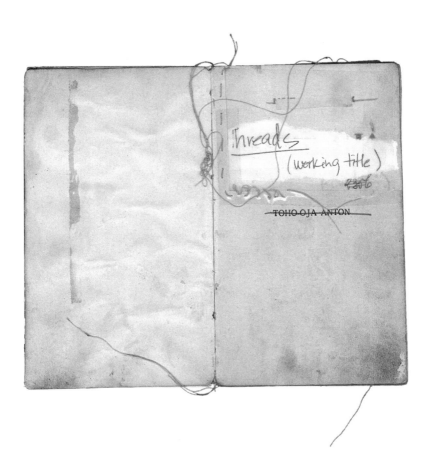

Threads
(working title)

TOHO OJA ANTON

A village is no longer a lane with trees and meandering fences, grazing, window boxes, private. Page after page of wheat turns in the wind alongside hungry apartment units.

Reading, I look away—

A small farmer who is not deported attempts adaptation while over time, the soil weakens. He resists by planting his own garden, after hours, and with her help.

(Dear Dad, if you can even vaguely translate—)

Why are you crying little flower

your buds full of tears?

Have you some heavy soulpain,

tender one, come to know?

Has Eesti ground (surface) spoken

silent night knowledge given

of ancient happy times,

of lost fortune declared?

Lift your head little flower!

Dawn has become Master!

His rays shiningly flashingly sending,

so that tears might dry!

As He noon-light scatters

over blooming (flowering) Eestiland,

oh, how we want to thank,

bloom, then in return, declare!

Roads spread legibly out from the old city into block apartment buildings of plastic perforated shoes, Russian. Her bunions and lack of citizenship, carrying a plastic bag and a satchel made of netting, radishes inside. I divert my eyes. I notice.

Where there is no landscaping or winding cobblestone streets, concrete stories absorb the residents who have made a pathway through the dirt to the bus stop versus the right angles of poured sidewalks

here, outskirts house forced migrations while the language exam is too difficult for citizenship and inconsistently scored.

Language classes, though expensive, are being offered as cases slip into a present continuous. I hope she is already coming. Russians are already there living. Passports are not being issued. Love is sometimes mixing Russian and Estonian, arranging thinking into new shapes.

Busses move the workers and unemployed through the outer grid, while inside the idea of sovereignty meanders through streets too narrow for ease.

The Gulf is crossed on high-speed ferries from salaries seven times higher toward cheap vodka, prostitution, leather goods.

State architecture falls from the brochure. Red tiled roof, red face, follow the umbrella. A flag on every corner. Toward which the photos lean.

Week four, my English drops into the dictionary's gutter like a city lost in the fold of the map. At the breakfast table of salty fish and boiled eggs, she asks, "Have you bananas in childhood?" and tells me of the difficulty of obtaining feminine products during Soviet times. Impossible not to imagine bloody rags as I slip into the fold. Her father argues that at least their pensions were secure.

The story is so—

of the Adventist Prophetess who is first a 19th-century New England schoolgirl, hit in the head with a stone thrown by another girl, and soon after, she has her first sacred visions. Continuing, in the early 20th century, missionaries go to Estonia where no religion has ever taken hold of the Estonian imagination but nationalism has, and the actor, my grandfather, converts and becomes a preacher after baptism by immersion in the Mother-river.

Later, "octobering" was encouraged as an alternative to baptism and preachers were deported.

If no stone then perhaps no need for exile. Follow this schema: because a stone was thrown.

Riverside, Feb.25,1975

Dear Mary and others,

Thank you for the check and a good letter.
We enjoyed to read it.

On 24th of February is the anniversay of Estonian
Republic, occupied now under Communists. The Cali-
fornia Estonéans SDA group gathered at Mrs. Elfriede
Einman's home, at Redlands, 13 persons, two were
missing. Dr. Hey preached about Israel, as they were
captove 400 years and Estonian; 800 years. They were
liberated by Moses, who liberates Estonian?

I spoke about the time of occupation and took
my album with me. Everybody enjoyed to look it as
the time of harshops of Estonians. I red also a
poem: I would take a bond of flowers
        and would tie you toketjer.
        Would tie you all together,
        O, my unhappy Estonia...

        I would take the blue of skies.
        Would take the shining sun.
        Would take the evening star and the d…
        for to tie you all together...

I would take the deepest love.
Would take the loyality an…
and would tie with th…
you, my beloved n…

        I woul…
        I …   …n,

                        …honesty,
                    … together
                …ve-land...

            …take the bonds of blood.
        …would take my brother's heart,
        and would tie with these you, together:
        O, my unhappy Estonia...

        Juhan Liiv,1864-1913   Tr. Ed.M.

We all cried as it was red...

And then we sung the Estonian antem led by a
record and Estonian male chorus.

"After a bombing we would hop on our bikes and go look for the damage."

"I thought the war was a game."

"Once a bullet came right through our window."

(Violent ear.

His stories in the ears to hum.)

In deer hunting season my brother and sister race ahead toward home. Whir of a bullet through the dry leaves above and running, my jacket flaps open.

Dear Grandmother: you fed yourself hard candies from a personal dictionary that snapped shut while slipping folded-up twenty dollar bills into my palms. His cast iron bookends. A file for every refugee he sponsored. Did you prefer Swedish to Estonian or English to Swedish and so on? Is there refuge? Your books in plastic covers. Your letters and rumors of poems.

—the work to disentangle myself from your illegibility

Sweeping up Tallinn windows shattered by bullets because a careless child left the light on. Making good use of every scrap of food. Keeping a can of money under the floorboards and in the night another son leaves. Radio reports, word of mouth, keeping house. It is safer if no one knows where.

Waiting for the missing is feminine and though the language is said to be devoid of gender, it is war.

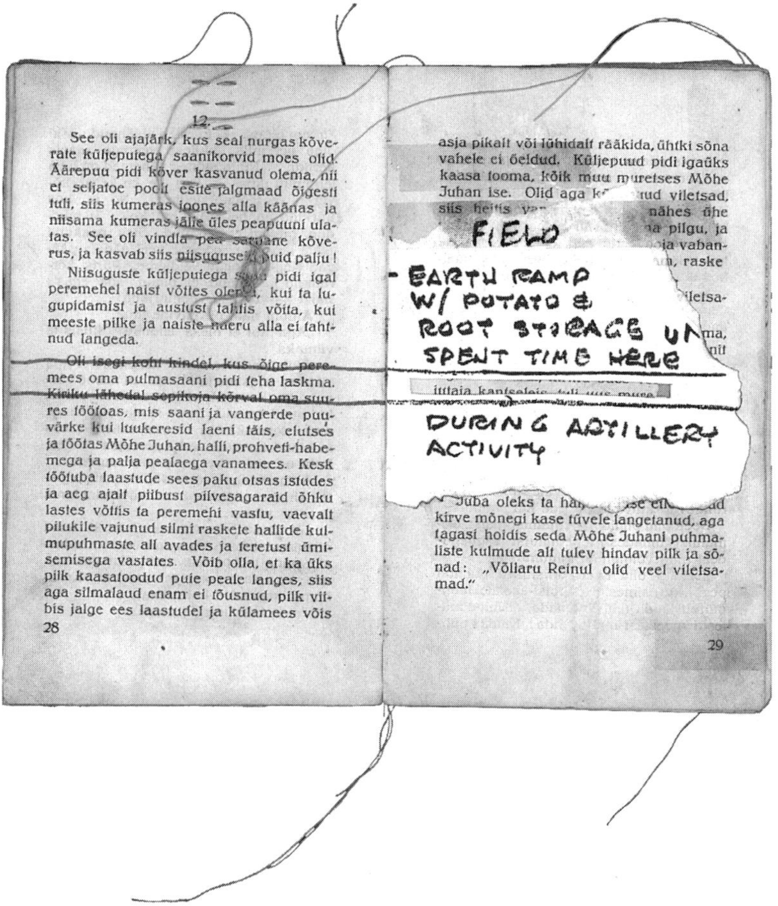

See oli ajajärk, kus seal nurgas kõverate küljepuiega saanikorvid moes olid. Äärepuu pidi kõver kasvanud olema, nii et seljatoe poolt esile jalgmaad õigesti tuli, siis kumeras joones alla käänas ja niisama kumeras jälle üles peapuuni ulatas. See oli vindla pea sarnane kõverus, ja kasvab siis niisuguseid puid palju!

Niisuguste küljepuiega saani pidi igal peremehel naist võttes olema, kui ta lugupidamist ja austust tahtis võita, kui meeste pilke ja naiste naeru alla ei tahtnud langeda.

Oli isegi koht kindel, kus õige peremees oma pulmasaani pidi teha laskma. Kiriku lähedal sepikoja kõrval oma suures töötoas, mis saani ja vangerde puuvärke kui luukeresid laeni täis, elutses ja töötas Mõhe Juhan, halli, prohveti-habemega ja palja pealaega vanamees. Kesk töötuba laastude sees paku otsas istudes ja aeg ajalt piibust piivesagaraid õhku lastes võttis ta peremehi vastu, vaevalt pilukile vajunud silmi raskete hallide kulmupuhmaste all avades ja teretust ümisemisega vastates. Võib olla, et ka üks pilk kaasatoodud puie peale langes, siis aga silmalaud enam ei tõusnud, pilk viibis jalge ees laastudel ja külameest võis

asja pikalt või lühidalt rääkida, ühtki sõna vahele ei öeldud. Küljepuud pidi igaüks kaasa tooma, kõik muu muretses Mõhe Juhan ise. Olid aga k[...]ud viletsad, siis heitis va[...] nähes ühe [...]na pilgu, ja [...]ia vaban[...]h, raske [...] [...]iletsa[...]ma, [...]nii

[handwritten note:]
FIELD
- EARTH RAMP
W/ POTATO &
ROOT STORAGE U[N]
SPENT TIME HERE

ittaja kantselei, tuli uus puna

[handwritten note:]
DURING ARTILLERY
ACTIVITY

Juba oleks ta hä[...]se el[...]ud kirve mõnegi kase tüvele langetanud, aga tagasi hoidis seda Mõhe Juhani puhmaliste kulmude alt tulev hindav pilk ja sõnad: „Võllaru Reinul olid veel viletsamad."

A successful bomb devastates the city's idea of itself. Now a footbridge, commemorating.

My obsession with the sounds of war—

Use the words you know for expressing direction to refresh

to unclose.

.

Late fall, sycamore tree bare. Thumping rush—

cloud of blackbirds. Sunday. Cold sky.

A small low-flying plane buzzes the house.

Blackbirds lift up again into a swarm and at seven years old

I wait for the whistling pitch of a falling bomb.

Fulcrum or inner fold:

that my father was born in Estonia and that both sides of my family adopted the 19th-century American religion, Seventh-day Adventism, a religion I no longer practice.

A language I do not understand.

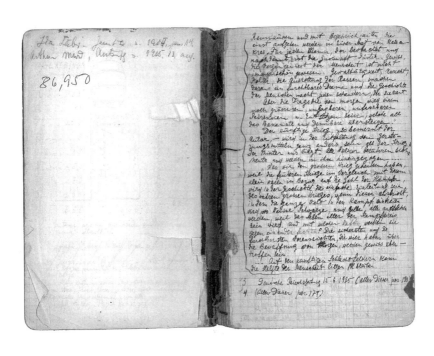

86,950

Rezensionen und mit Begeisterung aufgenommen werden in einer lage von Natur Krieg. Der jeden Menschen der beobachtet und nachdenkt, ist die Zukunft finster. Jenes die Sorgenzeit der Menschheit ist nicht immer schön gewesen. Gewalttätigkeit, Vernichtung, Folter, die Ausrottung der Rassen, machen daraus ein furchtbares Drama und die Geschichte der Menschen macht jeden schaudern. Wie sie nicht

Aber die Tragödie von morgen wird einem noch größeren, unfaßbaren, unfaßbareren Schrecken in Entsetzen sein, welche all das Bekannte und Denkbare übersteigen.

Der künftige Krieg, so bemerkt der Autor, — wird in der Entfaltung der Zerstörungsmitteln ganz anders sein, als der Krieg der hinter uns liegt. Alle Völker bewahren sich heute und werden in das hintergezogen ...

Das wir den großen Krieg geheißen haben, weil die früheren Kriege im Vergleich mit diesem klein sind, im Bezug auf die Zahl der Kämpfer, wird in der Geschichte die siebte Einleitung und des heben großen Krieges, wenn dieser ausbricht, in dem die ganze Welt in den Kampf eintreten wird so dass Schwarze und Gelbe, alle eingeschlossen werden, weil das Leben aller der Kampfpreis sein wird. Und mit welcher Waffe werden sie gegen einander kämpfen? Die sicherste und die furchtbarsten Neuerungsmittel, die wir heute über die Bewaffnung von morgen, werden gewiß eintreffen sein.

Auf den künftigen Schlachtfeldern kann die Hälfte der Menschheit liegen bleiben.

3 Deutsche Reichstagszeitung 15.6.1925 (aller Diener pag. 176)
4 (aller Diener pag. 179)

"Do not go to bars alone where you might get hurt

or worse yet, die."

"Because of our last name it would not be safe to go back."

With water on all sides, I approach

                              holding on

to the only guidebook and a dictionary where to weep is pronounced

nutma and wave is laine and threadbare is kulunud—

On the island I felt closer to fluency midagi (but) she mistook my Estonian for Finnish and when I pulled out Estonian money her face dropped, it being worth much less. Her granddaughter's English, intervening. I bought the sweater anyway and it never stopped smelling nagu (as) sheep but valuable.

The anthropologist from China explains the emptiness of her field research as our bus hurtles through forests of dense local knowledge, the sea visible from the road. Despite relative isolation, echt-culture slips through the years, over ceremonial cliffs, between waves. This social scientist's sullen face as she reports on the forgotten folk dances or perhaps their refusal to demonstrate a remembering.

Seabirds nest in rows of concrete bunkers, lookout towers rust.

Soviet antennas were not always so loosely attached.

First sighting of land. Everything is suddenly so full of this wind—

I ask. The answer is yes.

I am in a mirrorless room, startled by the self-portrait's seriousness.

Ferrying this return

                my own distance stood out more—

Where there are physical details to record such as the characteristics of buildings, tracing his movements over annotated maps, the shape of Russian cars or—

each day falls off into unspeech.

Overcome with German, he shouts "I feel younger since perestroika!"

Country of drunkenness, generous hair pomade,

stuttering infrastructure. It rains inside the café. Pulled, listening. Eyes

welling toward—

the spill on the edge of the table toward my notebook.

Backing away, "Thank you."

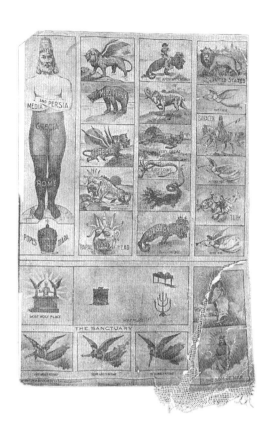

There are gloves decorated with designs or scarves and still other monuments. "I'm sorry, but we don't have any black shoes." Some having been torn down.

Now tourism looks inside restored churches and shops selling knit caps with long tassels. They try them on, laugh, not placing them carefully back, while previously, large busses pulled up to new monuments, unloaded, and gave a careful speech for a set price.

A certain degree of stiffness is usual. Gently ease open the boards by opening and shutting a little at a time. Take a couple of sections at a time from either end and gently press down, applying pressure on the spine.

Book cover: red smudges. Binding stitch pulled loose. Fabric edges, threadbare. It is not heavy and slightly larger than my palm. Black tape along the binding. Dictionary. Insert my grandfather's name here. His fingerprints. I flip through food stains at the corners, Estonian and English, without reading. A strand of hair falls from page two hundred and fifty-eight.

A citizen hobbles through the medieval city gate into the rebuilding. Crippled, his legs swing out to the side, his shoulders hunch and propel the weight of his legs, arms firmly placed inside the cuffs of the crutches as I watch. Because of The War: the reason I now assign to all injury.

I am able-bodied though heavy with a backpack, watching the walled city from the outside. Believing there is something to find out. A view called history. Or to enter.

This vertigo—

except the sounds of

his boyhood tones repeating the nine vowels, his development having remained—

looking up feels as though looking down on racing clouds. Mouth opened wide—

"And from the sea, the spire looks very imposing also."

I learn the principle of sound change as well as an extremely flexible word order.

Lined up behind a truck of provisions, women in kerchiefs turn away. For decades have been turning. I move the lens down from my face. Grey wisps our edges. They buy butter and bread or meat, freely, though expensive, and now, since The Singing Revolution, bananas.

Because of the cold, to wait (it's said that they wait), expect.

Sweden exiles Estonia sweetly, on the other side of perhaps—

will slowly free themselves.

"Look! There are a couple of novels on the table and the history of Europe is on the chair."

All the repairs to make because between the sea and the land is a line.

His scripts of autobiography shape

the sentence-rhythm of the seventh-day setting sun.

There is no retreat, perfect desk, binding tight, or right commentary while prayer has atrophied as the grammar-muscle of together. No particular blueprint. Map of comfort was—

Pillow of no tradition. Resting there.

palava ja niiske leitsega rammestavat rõh-
dumust sünnitasid. Alati hommikul, kui
tööle minnes uni silmist läinud, unustati
keskhommiku uinak, vaherati vikatit lui-
sates lauseid, jatkati lõunalaual arutu-
ng inimeste sarnasusest ja heideti õhtusõ-
oll gil ning põhku pugedes nalja inim-
liiks kude asjade üle, mis neilgi kahel vai-
va- võivat juhtuda.   nist,

7.

sieks
Anton arvas pulmad hiilsel sü-
gada- enne jõulu pidada. Küll peeti ka kev-
/älja, pulmi, olid isegi mõned perepojad
ides, kuul, valjuse, liliede, lehtede ja li,
laulu ajal, pikas rohes vedru vankrit
all, riku poole kihutanud ja esimest ööd n
kui naise kaskedega kaunistatud tahak-
et vil- risse ilma silma eest varjule viinud
anid ;
Aga hiline sügis oli viisipärasem ui ta
kohtumehest pererahele. Kogu veert
kõnna rikkamaid meeste tulefades eibhen-
nud ta kedagi, kes kevadel kosja
sõltnud. Sügisel olid oma nuumatud svae-
res veised hanid ja vähutav ning kä-
sest kesvavesi. Ja kuljuste ning aisaku-
se- helinal sõidetakse ilmatu pikas ron-
ste saanidega üle külmanud soode, lu-
hea tuisates ja ülemeelikute poiste uisa-
ise kirikusse.   sta
16

ia üle halja kaasiku ladva taeva sinasse
vahtida.
Eduard Magi ennem steste mõnu-

[handwritten text]
ees logelemiseks pidades,
ennast ühes oma perega laisklemiselt ta-
bada peljates.
Oldi imestanult liigutatud, kui pere-

THE STORY OF ELDER EDUARD MAGI

hena mõnele, kes ülekohut kannatanud,
kaitset kindlustas. Juleti kõvemini kõ-
nelda, Eduard and Liisa's Family se
raske rõhuvus, sai kuuldavaks inimeste
may be counted as follows

[handwritten text]
valju uks-
suse ja hirmul hoidva vaikuse halva-
muljet, mis Toho-ojal senni valit-
nud.
Oli tarvis tasuda Eduard Magiahkuse
julgustava naljaheitega mõndagi endi-
st ülekohtust.
THIRD SON:nd aru, mis mõju kurvas.
aljus, masinliku Tarmu Magirvapealsu-
ega töötavas peremehes selle muute oli
oonud? Kas aimasid nad, Jill Magi
19

Reflect that there are three statements of force concerning the thread.

A pull or tension unchanged.

A relation between the tensions of the two sides.

A force to feel, of generative tensions—

J. Mällo trükk, Tartus.

II. New York

1.

I've made artifacts with my hands like a trail of
„ussipärg" või „ubaleht", mis Toho-oia
breadcrumbs. To find a way back to a
päni, mõttekäigu kõrvale pööris ja kuju-
home I would have many lovers. A diaspora may
dakoelise uinutavilusa pildi kangastas.
be large and they make talk about which   pilk
iäi kahvatuisse ruutesse peatuma, mis
ones we should study. Or a diaspora may be inside
nisfanud, ja Anton tundis end vajuvat
one body of soula nd blood that hangs

See oli kui nägematu nõiavõimu küt-
onto the skin surrounding its quiet fragmentation.
vajumine.

This smaller spreading is my own and   ta
pilgu võluvalt pildiil, pühkis käega üle
my ears perk at the sounds of the larger. õrgust
vabaneda, tõusis üles ja katsus kaineile
mõttile virguda.

Aga uinakust oli jäänud ebamäärane
kaugusse kutsuv õnnetunne ja tuhmijoo-
neline tihedasse vinasse varjatud veetlev
pilt, nagu mälestus ununud aegadest.

5

To beat the odds of simultaneous death by bombing or arrest they slept in different root cellars. But not feeling this, presently—

the position of the single body versus a whole family.

Feel a map as the phenomenon of a ghost limb: then there is no loss.

Tell me again the story of everything depends on this I would be nothing therefore houses inside out as bodies also: "I once saw a smear of blood on the inside wall of a bombed-out house" stated as cool fact.

Dear Dad, we live in all topological dimensions at once—

SOMETHING LOOSE COULD FALL

sign on cracked city walls

color-coded flash cards
in my palms conjugate
to return

I DOUBT THE ACCURACY OF THIS MAP

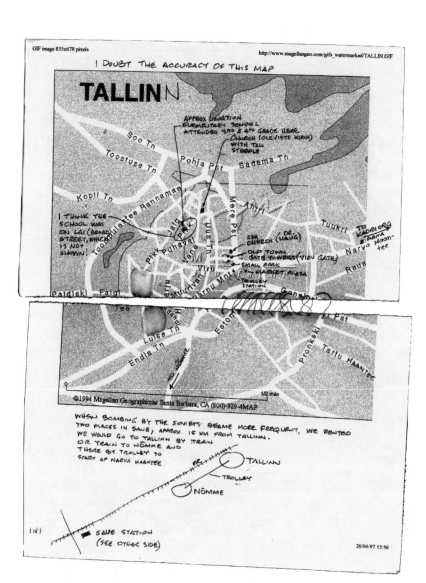

©1994 Magellan Geographix℠ Santa Barbara, CA (800)-929-4MAP

1/2 mile

WHEN BOMBING BY THE SOVIETS BECAME MORE FREQUENT, WE RENTED
TWO PLACES IN SAUE, APPROX 15 KM FROM TALLINN.
WE WOULD GO TO TALLINN BY TRAIN
OR TRAIN TO NÕMME AND
THERE BY TROLLEY TO
START OF NARVA MAANTEE

TALLINN
TROLLEY
NÕMME
SAUE STATION
(SEE OTHER SIDE)

1 of 1   26/04/97 15:56

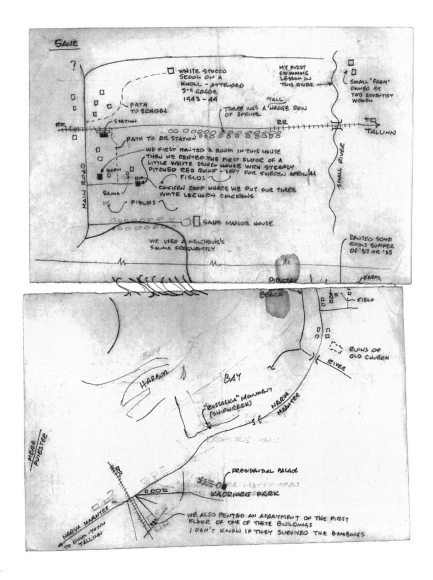

SAUE

?

WHITE STUCCO
SCHOOL ON A
KNOLL - ATTENDED
5TH GRADE
1943 - 44

MY FIRST
SWIMMING
LESSON IN
THIS RIVER →

SMALL "FARM"
OWNED BY
TWO ADVENTIST
WOMEN

PATH
TO SCHOOL

TALL
THERE WAS A 'HEDGE ROW
OF SPRUCE

RR

→ TO
TALLINN

STATION

RR

PATH TO RR STATION

WE FIRST RENTED A ROOM IN THIS HOUSE
THEN WE RENTED THE FIRST FLOOR OF A
LITTLE WHITE STUCCO HOUSE WITH STEEPLY
PITCHED RED ROOF - LEFT FOR SWEDEN APRIL/44

BARN

FIELDS

MAIN ROAD

SAUNA

CHICKEN COOP WHERE WE PUT OUR THREE
WHITE LEGHORN CHICKENS

WE   FIELDS

SAVE MANOR HOUSE

WE USED A NEIGHBOR'S
SAUNA FREQUENTLY

RENTED SOME
ROOMS SUMMER
OF '37 OR '38

SMALL RIVER

PIRITA

FARM

BEACH

FIELD

HARBOR

BAY

RUINS OF
OLD CHURCH

RIVER

"RUSSALKA" MONUMENT
(SHIPWRECK)

NARVA
MAANTEE

MÄRE
PUIESTEE

PRESIDENTIAL PALACE

KADRIORG PARK

NARVA MAANTEE

TO DOWN TOWN
TALLINN

WE ALSO RENTED AN APARTMENT ON THE FIRST
FLOOR OF ONE OF THESE BUILDINGS
I DON'T KNOW IF THEY SURVIVED THE BOMBINGS

Plaster falling away as skin from wood latticework

this city peels, its pages glued together by something personal
left inside the book.

Or neatly sutured.

Which roads lead out and which lead in?

No matter how many times I practice, mispronunciations tumble out of
necessity

crumble

to collapse

fate to hit, to fall upon

"So send this group of children home."

"Give me a package of envelopes."

"I'll write you a prescription."

German soldiers come down the road and ask my father, "Which way did the Russians go?" He points. Moments later, the Russians come through and ask, "Which way did the Germans go?" He points in the opposite direction.

My grandfather convinces German soldiers to let him use confiscated religious tracts for kindling. They agree, letting the charming Estonian take with him his volkgeist and bundles of publications back to the church from where they had just been seized.

Cleverness equals a national characteristic as they dream of being free, and, if under God, directly so.

In 1994 a Peace Corps volunteer finds a bronze church bell buried just under the forest surface during the last year of World War II to protect it from being melted into weapons. The President of Estonia donates one month of his salary to the people of Hiiumaa Island to restore the bell. Hearing this, the locals let it ring for Christmas then quickly take it down so that they will still get the money.

Postposition such as homeward

or sentences can occur apparently without a subject

and if you sit suddenly on nettles

this book is for learning Estonian

in the evening on one's knees.

Was completely silent.

Would I refuse to sing The Internationale

paint a blue watercolor picture for the word "sleep"

rip the star off the other child's shirt—

the last to pull the sled up the hill

                    both of us tiny for our age?

From which they fled,

       ·   light in the town of Haapsalu.

I slip between reeds as seabirds call up the names for Queen

Anne's lace, cattails, purple edge of horizon

                                    a space for thinking

and to walk. To inventory the weather and its colors where I do not

speak

while every word uttered in isolation is accented on the first syllable until

across the gulf he draws fluent arrows west.

1) Elas metsas muti onu
Keset kuuski noori vana
Kadaka põõsa juure all
Eluruum tal sügaval

2) Kutsus kokku külalisi
Karvaseid ja suleleid
Lendas vares harakas
Küll ja kaaren nupukas

3) Vantsis uhkelt karu lässa
Veeres siili okaskera
Läves nudisubaga
Orav kikkis karvaga

4) Laantes tuli välja põder
Hiljem jäi veel reinuvader
Kõik nad lauda istunud
Pidurooga maitsnud

5) Karu imes meekooki
Läves rüüpas kastejooki
Kaaren karumarju sõi
Küll see kurejooki jäi

6) Vares neelas lihatükki
Reinuvader kanakanti
Siil see aeani sugistas
Harakas häälega kekutas
                pööra

7) Põder limpsis sambla suppi
Orav näris käbijuppi
See oli päsa päeva aal
Pilla palla pillerkaar

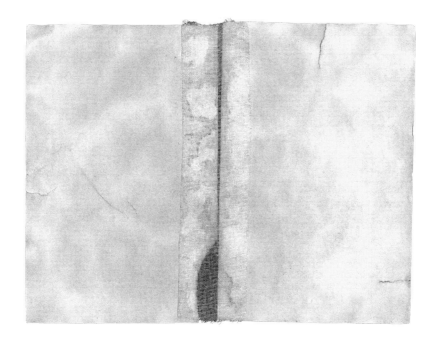

Care must be taken when sewing to place the needle

just under the fold—

avoid piercing the board paper—

Very little had been written on the construction of bindings.

Original is difficult. Longing, pronounced

igatsus is also yearning

for a Talking Book—

now "Saturday in the Sauna" is a short story

and there is still time until the evening

until the people began to write, singing,

original is still

there is time until the evening.

"Who is Estonian?" Folk songs, customary striped skirts and leather knickers, prettiest girls bloused in embroidery. Of course ribbons. "You emphasize especially the fine results achieved in wrestling and shooting."

She slices his picture from the page of the photo album and hands it to me, saying, "Here is your great-grandfather" "Doesn't he look like a Jew?" "Your grandmother, possibly she had some Jewish blood," "Her hair was not ever particularly light." Curly, yes or no. The name was Bloom or Blom or Blum and "Her grandfather was a tailor from Sweden so therefore." We use German. "Jovial also, that aunt, possibly part gypsy." "Certain professions or certain dispositions and fun-loving too." Saying "I am Jewish." Or not saying. "I am not Jewish." "I am Estonian." "A good bit of mixed blood."

To secure the proper papers awaiting deportation or to flee, scrambling for identities, against—

"What is your nationality, Miss?" "Really? I thought you were French." "Because (this is because) I am from—" His accent and not myself. "This is because my nose is not or my ears are so or not as blonde as my sister" and "the Estonian's humor is particularly dark."

To watch suspicions unfurl.

To pull a smile from the waiter is my foreignness.

His hair falling across my pillow, map of a river delta.

While I could not sleep.

Ghostly national imaginings float down on top of the fabric of longing as coffee slips out of the cup carelessly served.

Finally I managed to find you, versus. Emphasis mine.

mitte nüüd, uuesta nälja järu
ma olen väsinud, Jumal.

5) Kui tuleb veotus, muu rimbeterele,
kui müürsk plaksvatel ja valgus
sähvatel, siis taan selgesti
et varsti olen surnud. Isand
ma olen väsinud.

6) See polnud elu, mis mina
plaanetesin. Ma ei mõelnud
Vitnami. Aga kui peaps maailma
le tuleme rahu.
Minu elu ei antud, aga mitte
asjata. Ma olen väsinud
Jumal, ag nitte ja tulf
koju.

palu iiks teine päevan an täis
võitlust ja ta plust

The door was opened.

The Singing Revolution was bloodless.

Before love, grace, mercy. One must choose. Sõda or sõja

is war according to the rules.

Mr. Gorbachev: thank you for your glasnost.

Photocopying tightly controlled, their books typed and re-typed through stacks of carbon paper, hand-bound bindings loosen under coats or in baskets under turnips or carrot greens, under mattresses.

Pass the book on to the next person in exchange for—
hunger and trust

is to read.

Legal books with colorful cover art, clean type, opaque pages now stacked quietly for sale, their bindings tight next to the roar of history. Next to doctrines made of translucent paper, weak spines, to be touched.

snowstorm, tramping in deep snow up to his hips, sometimes in rainstorms, wet to the neck. Sometimes he was treated well in the best homes of our members, sometimes he had to stay at poor members in an unheated room and to shiver all night in his cold bed. Usually, he never used hotel rooms, also there were none in the small villages. Sometimes he had to stay overnight in the loft of a born, where the horses and cattle crackle for their food all the night through and the smell of the cattleshed was the air to breathe. While traveling several times the motorcycle of his co-workers dropped into the ditch while he sat on the back of it, hurting his ailing back again and again. But the destination had to be reached. . .

He has preached the Adventist message in halls of a thousand seats and also in small cottage meetings or farmhouses or to 3-5 persons only. In many farm meetings the dogs growled under the seats of women, interrupting the speech. Usually, the speaker then said: "I do not understand how to talk to the dogs, please lead them out and then I may continue again!" This remark woke up the sleepy listeners and the talk continued again.

Elder Magi was one of the best speakers in the Estonian Conference, winning during his ministry more than 700 souls to our beloved message. As he had also a talent of singing and had studied music with three professors, very often he sang himself at his public meeting gospel songs, lifting up the souls to Christ.

Almost in every city he preached and had energetic meetings, an opposition arose. In Tartu, a team of Lutheran pastors and ministers of Baptists and Methodists was organized to supress the SDA message. Our team was: Elders D. N. Wall, Ehrhard from America and E. Aug and E. Magi of Estonia. The meetings were same theater where Elder Magi formerly played as an actor and where he mentioned before. A good number of precious souls were baptized and the Advent truth was victorious again!

(next page)

"Keegi ei taha surema" is no one wants to die

and when passive there are endings

you must apply

such as -kse

as in "Mida siin tehakse?"

               What is being done here?

There is no past tense in the grammar of telling

in Estonian there is no then or there,

it is only here.

To dwell, live, stay.

To settle one's mood since beginning from alone,

a state.

A book is not held together by thread alone: the strain is relieved by backing, linings, board positions and, in some degree, its covering.

The thickness of thread is selected so that the resulting swell in the spine is taken up by—

gravity will affect the sewing and the threads will loosen.

Eventually the sewing breaks down and the binding collapses.

seid painutatud, nüüd pidi ta saani kü̈e
jepuu kõlbulikuks aitama teha. Lõgli
uued obadused paine otsie juure ja eema̱a̱
mõõdeti ja joosti toa vahet.

Katlasse pisteti kõlbmatu küljep vast
lasust eda. Antsule näis see nii prak-
kastami korraks vurrudki fend uruks,
varisele siibadena tõusid. Aga ha puu
gesani, arsti — p ak mehe bt nägu
süg mie pilves il ise ele il rele tar-
thikt aurupilv katidas oli põl-
mal miast välja, ora detuiuüülje, nagu
Paa kõlbammuga unnu i pa e je
tis üüd otsa pae mat u a oba ar vahtis
heisinng hakk ja mi ol ı all a järsu
Antus argas apõlbm kah ktmehuucorvale
küljma u pikemtut ksa peafe s ke asiku

nud vaatlikul ikkan sil" n
peraadies, ja ædjuamõõc i vi pime puu
altat lible. Juba R see nitanadili mialaja
nulb-ojale võis la h ja enien airtaks ̄aagu
ei ja jäkinud sust da. Atds vae ol pe
metus boole ja vsurud häd kasid ousma
agæd...ton jät töleseks st s

Kas vajutas nüüd Ants korrans
järsku, või pragises koor paindumi
kohutas painutajaid, aga järsku kãa
puu paine ja obaduste vahelt väljı
mehed kukkusid kãpili.

60

24.

Oodati põnevusega Antoni otsustamist.
Teda oli alati eeskujulikuks meheks pee-
tud, nüüd pidi ta eeskujuliku sammu
astuma.

Aga missugune samn oleks eest u
julik? Missugune samn on ten̄ı vı an
line?

Selle
E ni̇̄sukesu
ata jätab!
uk foa-
n rtuks.

se sa.
Pri jısı
ja

ma,
bıuen

mına ka
kosja s-
dass."

„Oless ja oless!... Mis-sa nüüd siss
niisuke ei ole!"

63

I read a fading "CCCP" across cracked walls. The red letters of Olympic uniforms. A dog snarls, pushing me back. Into safety. Into thoughts of Olga Korbut who was not so Soviet, they said, smiling. He pointed out the Estonian names among the basketball players. I pointed out the missing lines on each map and globe, the meaning of defect.

Mismatched uniforms, the border patrol boat on display, marching past photos of the new army. His red steep roof noted on the map, to find. The train window spreads my reflection across collective farm equipment, rusting.

CHICKEN COOP

WHERE WE PUT

OUR THREE WHITE

LEGHORN CHICKENS

LEFT FOR SWEDEN APRIL '44

A child holds balloons. Comforted, before leaving.

"I'll wait for you," he said, "this far," then going away.

An engineer leans into me, alcohol on his breath, offering

a walking tour and a Victory Day bonfire.

I use German to refuse.

Many precious photos, parts of which have been cut out with scissors or some faces which have been changed beyond recognition through scratches or smears—

—were directed to snitch from photo albums directly and indirectly incriminating pictures.

The compiler and writers find it necessary to point out that the book of records is far from perfect.

Where my name is popular like Smith rather than mispronounced they ask

"Know you eesti keel?" the Estonian tongue, though the missionaries and anthropologists were German, giving the language its shape. Giving pianos, blackboards, seashore, culture, church, demanding a Bible for the Undeutsche.

Monuments to the battles on the island of Saaremaa have numerous placards reading Mägi as members of both armies. I make a pencil rubbing of various conscriptions in one family and the loss of an umlaut.

Travel to The West was granted only in extreme cases ("when she was on her deathbed, my sister,") and a training seminar was mandatory. Instruction on what to take pictures of: railroad stations, highways, airports, information on phone lines, dialing. If you were to build a house it could not be so large as to be anti-communist. He uses German to explain that it was in the '70s. In 1991 tanks rolled into the streets, the tension building, but he survived, the cramping and shooting pain was a heart attack, this deep desire for peace.

Take a tour of Estonian farmers, their horses now pulling rakes.

Was in prison or arrested, yes. Of whom to trust—

Bus station engines backfiring, audible gasps, having witnessed—

Only the smokestacks and smoke are visible.

deported and killed. The great de[
night of June 14, 1941. It was so
midnight everywhere the Russians [
pack some luggage and took the [rtation of Estonians occurred in a secret
by deporting the arrested to ra[secretly arranged over all the country, that at
loaded on the cattlecars, wat[[r]acked the homes, giving only 20 minutes to

Luckily, they did not look [[fam]ilies or singles to a waiting and armed truck,
in his office on a sofa and [[rail]way stations. There the families were separated and
sent for safetys' sake to an[by Russians, waiting for transport.

Attending the Sabbath m[[Thi]s first night for Elder Magi. He was sound asleep
he learned what had happe[room was closed by a steel-door. His family was
Lord! After the service[[anot]her city.
were arranged, packed [[morn]ing service, he noticed the church was in tears. There
certain purposes. Th[the past night. And he was saved! Thanks be to te
people cried for he[he went to the railway station. The trains of cattlecars
every car. Nobod[with arrested Estonians. Only a hold in the corner for
nowwhere - to a[small window, fenced. The doors scarcely opened. The poor
They were Est[and water in the hot summer day. The Russian soldiers watched
government [[w]as permitted to approach. Next night, the trains rolled to
was [ai[[Si]berian slave camp in the woods or mines. What were the accusations?
[the [[ma]ns. They were national people. They were farmers. They were
[con]ferenc[[offi]cers, preachers, "capitalists" and - <u>Anticommunists</u>, as every Estonian
to tell [still is.

at that same night, Eduard escapted the city. Only one devoted man knew where the
Meete president escaped. "The President is visiting churches," he was permitted
Commun[But which ones, that he did not know. There were 44 churches in Estonia
separ[time.
char[[tak]ing his family in another town, he took them to a secret farm while the
fa[[communi]sts and Nazis had battles about in the same area. They slept every one in a
[separ]ate area to avoid a full arrest of the family. Two men watched the place by
[chan]ging the post every two hours. There were five of the Magi family, plus the
[fam]ily members of the farm.

(next page)

8

The bombing of two enemies was near to this farm. A river was between
them. A brand new bridge was blown up by the Russians. Schrapnel flew
over the farm yard. Everyone hid themselves in a deep potato cellar
under a strong barn. The cellar had a front room and a second room, both
protected by heavy doors because of winter cold. Straw and hay was laid on
the potatoes and the "beds" were ready for everybody in a large room. The
shells hit the door and ceiling, but the place was safe. One night, as the
bombing had a pause, the farmer and Elder Magi left the cellar to see if
any fire has started in some houses of the farm. Suddenly a shell flew
so close at Elder Magis ear that he felt the heat and the whistling sound
of it . . .Too close!

During this first Russian occupation, the brother of Mrs. Magi was brutally
killed as a former police officer. His wife with teenaged children were
all deported to Siberia, where the mother and son died in the hard work at
slave coal mining camp. A number of Adventists suffered too, by deportation
killed by bombs and forcefully put to serve in the Russian army, among them
also a young Bible worker of the church.

The conference office had to work very, very carefully. By a strong and
foreful way, one of the committee members was set to spy on the President
and the committee. He had to report every week the work of headquarters.
Nobody except the conference president knew, that he was the "spy," because
they both were the best friends and co-workers for the Lord. They meet and
write now sometimes here in USA, to each other.

Now, as at the mentioned farm where Magis hid themselves, the Russians
noticed a very strong horse was hidden behind the housrs. A Russian officer
noticed it and came to the farm to confiscate the horse. The farmer told
tolder in Estonian, let's attack the man and kill him. Elder Magi ad
him to handle the case in a friendly way. Let him have the horse, and I
Mag will ask the Russian officer to give to the farmer a tired horse.

(next page)

Ema is mother (easily formed) and emajogi is the Mother-river and there

they were baptized but I am not

while isa is father (a higher register.)

Isamaa being literally fatherland but the small step between mother and

earth (maa) softens this. Try to say

tütretütar, daughter's daughter,

as in modern Estonian there is not always a single word

for each relative.

To copy the sounds, I blur my eyes.

Between his heart and throat I would nestle myself.

Try to say it: õunapuu is apple tree and the tigu climbs up.

I enter the building as the daughter of one who left, slip money into the machine and press against the binding. The librarian hands over the heavy book published "to settle history." Blom, Blum, Bloom: my finger follows columns of "deported and dead or missing." Light crosses each page and I leave with reproductions of reproductions of arrest documents on paper longer than the U. S. standard letter.

"My good friend and philanthropist Eduard Magi." Some years later he had changed his beginning in the letters as follows: "My good friend and BROTHER Eduard Magi! He had accepted the Advent truth and had become a member of the church. Later, he became a teacher in Sabbath school and still later was ordained to be a deacon of the church in this home of seniors. Now he sleeps in peace. He never was able to meet his wife, who was not permitted to leave Russia. She had to stay in Moscow. With the assistance of Eduard Magi and an American friend, she was sent a sewing machine to help earn her living in Russia.

Another interesting occupation story: February 24 is the independence day of the Estonian Republic, since in 1918 she declared her independence from old Russia. This independence was tramped under their feet first by the Rus~ the Germans, then by the Germans and a second time by the Russians ~ation of the Germans wanted to s~ ~ ~ ~ before the powers of the world and organized a friendly meeting on Estonian Independence Day, February 24, 1944 in the Estonian capitol in a large concert hall, where the Adventists formerly had held their large conference meetings. The Nazis forced all the churches of the city to come to these meetings and to bless the Estonian flag as a "Flag of victory."

The Estonian flag has three colors: blue, black and white. Blue is their sky, black their fruitful soil and white their conscience in history.

At this meeting, the Lutheran archbishop talked about love and blessed the flag in the Luthern way. The Metropholit of the Orthodox church sprinkled the holy water on the flag according to their custom. The Catholic Nuncios, blessing the flag, praised the blue color of the flag, as the blue color of the dress of the Holy Mary; the minister of Methodists prayed for the "victory flag, and then came the turn of the Adventists to bless the flag, as the last speaker. It is always the best to be a last speaker. Elder Magi took a text in Acts where it is told by Paul of the freedom of nations and of the way of the Lord

(next page)

From far away.

Soul to bury.

I can't breathe anymore.

To sprinkle. I'll sprinkle some cold water on you

to rescue—

clever (leaving, to save)   though clear regret.

Blue sea, clear sky, fresh air. I don't regret coming here.

Other prisoners sew my poems in their clothes.

But they were sent there for hiding me in their farm.

I had no right to ruin their lives.

I built my bunker on the latticework ceiling.

A learned man, a lost letter.

A mouth stuffed with clouds.

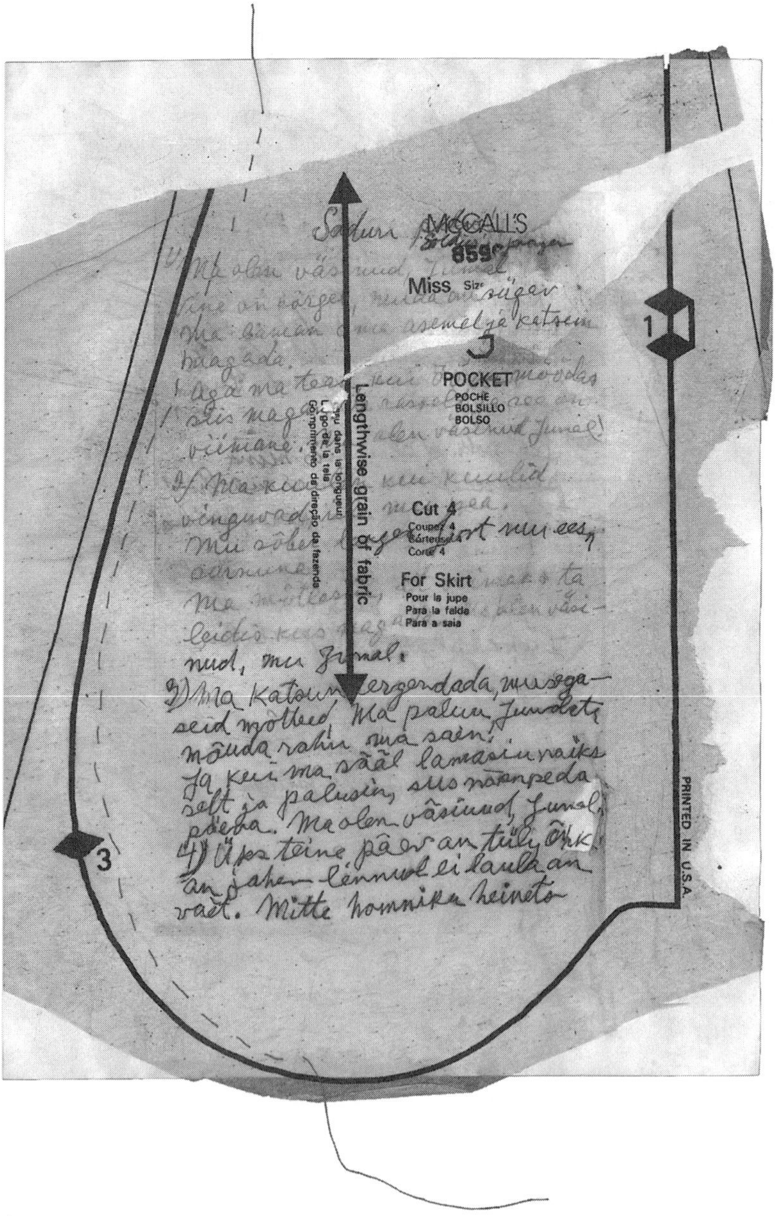

McCALL'S
8599

Miss Size

POCKET
POCHE
BOLSILLO
BOLSO

Cut 4
Coupez 4
Cortense 4
Corte 4

For Skirt
Pour la jupe
Para la falda
Para a saia

Lengthwise grain of fabric

1

3

(Handwritten Estonian text, partly illegible:)

Sakuri

1) Ma olen väsinud, Jumal
jõud on otsas, nüüd sügav
ma ainsas oma asemelje ketsem
magada.
Ja ei ma tean nii moodes
1) atis magha,
viisiaine. en väsinud Jumal)

2) Ma tean kei kuulid
vingivader. mu sõber la get mu eesq
Ma leidis kes mag ta len väi
leidis kes mag
nud, mu Jumal.

3) Ma katun ergendada, musega—
seid mõtheed. Ma palun Jumaleti
mõnda rahu ma saen?
Ja kui ma sääl lamasin naiks
selt ja palusin, sus nõmpeda
päeha. Ma olen väsinud, Jumal.

4) Üps teine päev an tüli õnk
an jahan lennul ei laulan
vael. Mitte hommika heinetõ

Dear—

I found the poems by Gmother we talked about. In translating them, I took some "poetic" liberties with English grammar and syntax, as you will notice. In doing so, I felt I was able to convey some of the mood and rhythm of the original language. I also found a sheet of paper with the translation of the Estonian national anthem and a poem by Lydia Koidula on it. The latter I attempted to translate quite literally. The word "isamaa" in literal translation is "fatherland." But "fatherland" sounds too tough, too robust in English, maybe too Germanic. To the Estonian mind "isamaa" is more tender and loving than "fatherland." Thus "native land" seems a more appropriate translation. Besides, self-respecting Estonians would not, God forbid, be identified with Germans, although they are a mixed race with a good dose of German blood in them. I also found the copy of a letter from Gfather with a translation of another Estonian poem in it. The poet—Juhan Liiv—incidentally attended the same high school in Tartu that I did, although he did it 100 years earlier. Juhan Liiv's poems are very melancholy. He suffered from depression and eventually committed suicide.

Greetings to you and J.

Love—

"The grandchildren" (we) "only point at me when—"

this I am told she wrote in letters from (my) America

sometimes in code (the use of certain Bible verses)

responding to preprinted Soviet envelopes but

Estonia has now gone over to the common Western style

and would not write Dear unless they meant it.

One who comes.

One who washes.

Who wishes.

Seer, prophet.

One who is dying.

One who is doing.

Rummaging through boxes of my anxiety in the basement looking for his naturalization papers for many years we call him "a man without a country" and he always answers "don't make fun of the poor refugee," laughing. The meaning of natural.

näitas Anton, et tä ei olegi nii igav, et ta naljagi mõistab heita ja lõbusaid lugusid puhuda, mis kohvilauale ja pühapäeva-õhtusele videvikule kohased.

Laskis isegi mõne noole, mille sihtjoont ainult alguses märgata võis, langemise koht aga vaevalt aimatav oli.

Siiski võis vallavanem aimata eelolevaid sündmusi ja Truuta vahekorda peakohtumehega.

Lahkumine sündis tulevalgel, kus kambri soojus ja elevus hingedes kõik oli lähendanud; suruti tugevasti käsa ja lubati palju silme- ja näoilmega.

18.

Järgmisel hommikul tõusti vara ja jõuti metsataalude väljadest üle, enne kui kellegi silm veel nägemas.

Ants ei tunnud peremeest ära, nii lõbusas tujus oli see, kandis kahe r. he leivakotti ja astus nii kiiresti ees, et järele sai lipata.

Mindi seekord kaugemale, lasti otse mööda laiu sihte kahe okaspuu müüri vahel lääne poole, peatati alles keskhommikul ja võeti enne tööle hakkamist linnupetet.

„Noh Ants, kui ia küllepuu leiad, võtame sulle kah naese," ütles Anton.

44

„Sometimes I wish ████ was thick;iksid naeru pärast kinni, suu lahti, vurrud tõusand I wish ████ I wish I had ad üles.

smooth and ████?"

Kurku ummistava naeru või nutu läbi

████ I took my weight

„Kis minusugusele ka tuless..."

into cafes and restaurants,s tüdrukid küll!

Ma lään isi sulle isamehest."

Not tall and wispy like a birch tree,d metsa, igaüks oma mõtetega.

or a strand of ████ vahtis Anton põneva tähelpanuga läbi tüvede sam-Solid and wide like an oak. ████ na tagant tabada püüdes ja metsa kiiresti a long time to move, that decisions to go meant kõrvale põigates ja rägastikkudest rüseeveryone around would have to readjust.

Siis seutas uks oksadest ja raagu-And ████ warmth and mass tuse nõialaterna, ja selle valgusel hakkas ta and ████ home would shrink and ████.

See oli ühel kevadisel päiksepais-would say ████ something's missing, udav niiske soojus hõljus, soos samblakord juba kuiv all sulanud, aga kelts veel tee kohal käijaid kandis.

Nad tulid Truutaga kahekesi üle välja koolitoa juurest alla soo poole, Antonil

45

Children take me to their barn, singing. Holding my hand, the first
touch—

"related" translates

gotten (of the language.)

(Of the milk.) (Of the barn.)
(Of the soul is the country.)

Singing far enough into the countryside where it is peaceful.

My open smile even if for the photo I am seated next to the man of a
distant relation who came back from a work camp barely upright, sipping
milk and soup in his pajamas and a metal frame bed for seven years.

Of buttermilk curdling further.

Kitchen flies and cut hay.

Homemade cottage cheese and chestnuts.

"How does your hand go?"

(How are you?)

Of the foot, atrophied.

Of timid.

Of wet.

Of the skin he lets, he weeps.

"Please give me milk soup."

Two ways of treating the first and last sections—

however, if the thread is pulled too tightly the spine becomes concave and difficulty is experienced in backing. The same is done on the completion of sewing, when the endpaper thread is hooked around the previous two sections.

Tallinn light past ten. Vined walls. Split gardens.

Sun-darkened face wedged into a corner

knees pull up into—

(yellowing, my itinerary)

his white hair, wild

arms murmur around—

a dusky transition to capitalism.

Siis on ta nende kõikide sarnane, n[i]
sama õnnelik, niisama joobunud, niisam[a]
nõrk.

Aga ei, ta ei ole ometi nende sarnan[e.]
Ta ei taha nende sarnane olla !

Siiski, lõõtsapilli kaeblikud helid teeva[d]
teda nõrgemaks, murravad, painutav[ad]
muljuvad ja vintsutavad. See õhkki[!]
joovastav, uimastav ja nõrgestav.

Ta tõuseb püsti.

„Lähme vist ühes koju poole," [ü]tl[eb ta]
Truutale.

Ja nad lähevad pimedal sü[gi]s[e] õhtul
ühes minema.

Antonil tuleb meele viimase päeval
koolist kojuminek.

Täna on raskem rääkida, on ka nii
vähe öelda.

Kui mehiselt ta siis jumala[ga] jättis ja
sirgelt koju poole sammus kindel olles,
et Truuta talle korragi järele vaatab.

Enne Tülba õue väavasse jõudmist
on kõik öeldud, mis tarvis.

Ja Truuta on, oma hääles nukrust var-
jamata, tema otsuse õigeks tunnistanud.

Nad suruvad tugevasti teineteise kätt
ja Anton on kindel, et Truuta talle kor-
ragi järele vaatab.

Aga näeb ta pimeduses, kui mehiselt
ja sirgelt Toho-oja Anton koju poole sam-
mub? Ainult jalad nõtkuvad põlvist; aga
selle eest on südames tundmus, et ta tu-
gev on, tugevam kui need teised.

(Dear Dad, if you can even vaguely translate—)

Songs (laulud) tears are always

secret heart droplets always.

Be it mighty painful urge (drive)

be it tender feeling of happiness.

Movement of a little spring,

movement of a little droplet,

wave breaks freely,

its melody gives good feeling—

does its spray spread on cliff?

(do its droplets swell on cliff?)

Are they guarded by forest grayness?

When does tongue question this?

Flow, now, song-water!

Move, kind wavelet!

Ja (and) when your light (sprightly)

wings to someone's eyes

kindness (sprightly) carries,

then I want to remain at peace.

English and Estonian mix now with German, a nation blurs so—

the "Mond ist schön" were my first German words though

I have forgotten which article.

Can you praying? Can you German? Can you Estonian?

Can you staying?

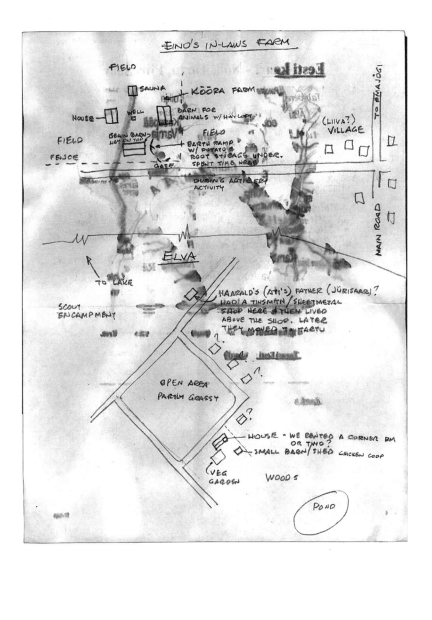

EIND'S IN-LAWS FARM

FIELD

SAUNA   KÕÕRA FARM

House   WELL   BARN FOR
                         ANIMALS W/ HAYLOFT

FIELD   GRAIN BARN   FIELD
         HAY ON TOP
FENCE   EARTH RAMP
                         W/ POTATO &
              GATE   ROOT STORAGE UNDER.
                         SPENT TIME HERE
                         DURING ARTILLERY
                         ACTIVITY

(LIIVA?)
VILLAGE

TO EMAJÕGI

MAIN ROAD

ELVA

TO LAKE

SCOUT
ENCAMPMENT

HAARALD'S (ATI'S) FATHER (JÜRISAAR)?
HAD A TINSMITH/SHEETMETAL
SHOP HERE & THEN LIVED
ABOVE THE SHOP. LATER
THEY MOVED TO TARTU

?

?

OPEN AREA
PARTLY GRASSY

?

?

HOUSE - WE RENTED A CORNER RM
                    OR TWO?
SMALL BARN/SHED CHICKEN COOP

VEG
GARDEN   WOODS

POND

In the forest "es gibt ein Lager," she said.

"It's not unusual for the older generation to be quite comfortable speaking German." Her grammar was better than mine.

I hear history

rather than summer camp, tents, happily green.

"We had no idea about them."

    —howls the quiet, the night

        looking for cement footings, feeling, I did not stay.

The night is night is history   knowing. We tried to put our arms around the largest tree but our fingers never touched on the way to the Lager.

As the method of sewing restricts the movement of the sections, rounding is sometimes difficult but will be achieved by perseverance.

To keep the spine pliable—

All along, sewing a section along its length with one piece of thread.

Birch starkly white-lit all night. Sketching a window.

Made of birch twigs for the bathhouse,

take it, here's the whisk.

To steam,

to soothe.

Sketching a breath a fingerprint dissolves.

Phrasebook marked here.

I am

hello. My name unfolded from a backpack tightly.

Hair smelling of travel and heat as if honey—

sweeter also than honey from the honeycomb

I fall into the Psalms.

Your room here though water pressure not strong and breakfast at that

time, yes.

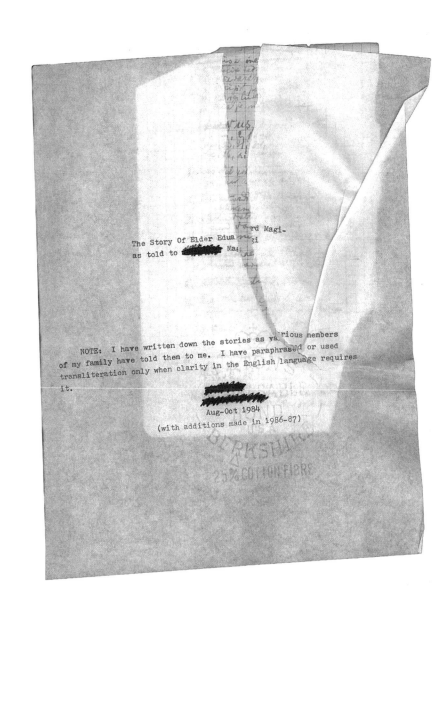

The Story Of Elder Edua...rd Magi-
as told to ████████ Ma...

NOTE: I have written down the stories as va...rious members
of my family have told them to me. I have paraphrased or used
transliteration only when clarity in the English language requires
it.

████████
████████

Aug-Oct 1984

(with additions made in 1986-87)

About the prickerbushes snagging my ski jacket then

this night

June brightly unpacking

his stories by nightlight

in June those yellow—

           not freesia

           yes honeysuckle—

narrating this night I find that word about this flower.

(Dear Dad, if you can even vaguely translate—)

(Oh) Returning Home from Afar (Kaugelt Koju Tulles)

Eesti bread, only one that tastes sweet to me—

Eesti borders, only one that securely protects me—

I could not suffer any longer!

Oh, how cold strange foreign sun shines!

Foreign tongue—how stiff it sounds!

Everywhere I saw you, I heard,

foreign singers I heard plenty—

Vanemuine's (god of song)

children's harp song(s)

no one knew—that is when I cried:

"Home again I want to travel!"

I carry my father's body through a forest. He is hollow—

I step through ferns thickly and over fallen trees, soft rot beneath.
Carefully.

Light slowly building, smell of green.

A body's heaving silences read as

to be leaving.

The last Estonian guerrilla fighter was chased out of the forest decades after the end of The War. Beard and fingernails long. Farmers fed him, the last of The Forest Brethren. He drowned trying to cross a small pond.

So much should not be spoken.

One shouldn't get up so early.

May this book not be read.

ar. It was a hard time for Mrs. Magi! The newly elected

had done for the Estonian Conference left also soon for Germany, Elder R. V.
to the North
to the Gene his family. They are also now in the U.S.

a life-lon Eduard Magi received a year's vacation from the General Conference,
and, th
learned the (Swedish) language. He worked also for Estonians in Stockholm
ad was appointed by the Swedish Conference to minister to a Swedish church in
Orobro, which he called his "best church" in all his service for the Lord in any
land.

One day in Sweden he received a telegram from Skodsborg Sanitarium from
Dr. Anderson, who had a letter from his oldest son from France, where he was
located during the end of the war. The lost son was found! The Skodsborg Sanit-
arium helped us again! "A heavy stone is lifted from my heart," said his mother
But we could not yet meet him. That happened some years later in Amer

In 1946, the General Conference called Eduard Magi t well-being after
to become pastor of the Estonian-Russian-Ukranian called without ever seeing
the U.S. he attended the seminary at Takoma Par in Moscow all her life.
in New York City, in the Bronx and Manhatten arranged to send her a sewing
meetings in the Academy of Music in the in Stockholm, I received a year
Elder Magi received many good words of Conference. I soon learned the
He also advertized the Estonian meet ish church in Orebro, which was
to the Estonian meetin in Manhatten All my service for the Lord in any
language!

Coming from the old country to and a letter from my oldest son, Eino,
It follows him everywhere! Elder where he had ended up at the end of the
it is much closer to him with the My wife said "a heavy stone has been
The second World War create saw each other again in America, years
Adventists who were in the camp
wrote to these camps for inform Russian-Ukrainian Church in New York City.
and neighbor states to find pe to the US on the ship MV Gripsholm, which

In the present tense rings of brown line teacups. I collect stains and bits of leaves. Bus stop below, coming and going. Iron gates and lace over shutters. The subway shakes the windows as again you don't arrive so I wait, rumbling, an inherited map.

.

Kuldne kodukotus

I flip through pages as told, not knowing the numbers called out until the music begins and the hymn's chords are legible so it is possible to sing the wrong words. Her warm breath, consonants popping next to my ear: "He is saying 'he was a great man' so please stand, his daughter-daughter." Earphones for the Russian speakers hang in the last two rows of pews reserved, "but they should learn" is the other side of the debate behind the glass, translating.

Boys and girls test their English with "super" and their "yes" is deliberate, preceding each attempt at a sentence. I write down names in a small reporter's notebook. "Take greetings back, please."

Petals fall from flowers daily

soon—

Yours—

On the other side of the glass, you walked away.

Now tea glasses sweat, rattle in their metal holders toward Riga
on slow tracks.

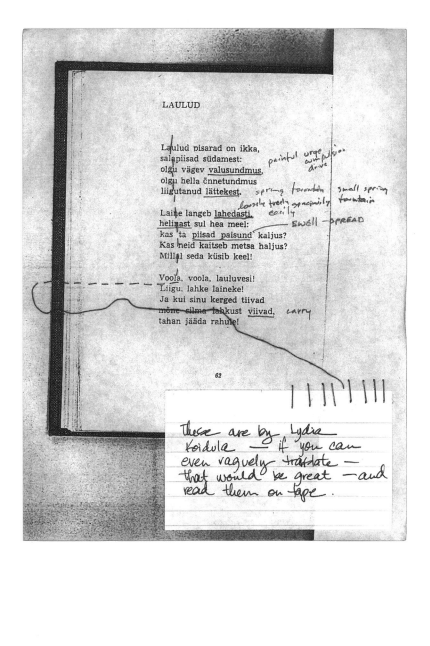

LAULUD

Laulud pisarad on ikka,
salapiisad südamest:
olgu vägev valusundmus,
olgu hella õnnetundmus
liigutanud lättekest.

Laine langeb lahedasti,
helinast sul hea meel:
kas ta piisad paisund kaljus?
Kas neid kaitseb metsa haljus?
Millal seda küsib keel!

Voola, voola, lauluvesi!
Liigu, lahke laineke!
Ja kui sinu kerged tiivad
mõne silma lahkust viivad,
tahan jääda rahule!

62

[handwritten annotations:] painful urge / compulsion / drive · spring fountain · small spring fountain · loosely freely spaciously easily · SWELL—SPREAD · carry

[handwritten note:] These are by Lydia Koidula — if you can even vaguely translate — that would be great — and read them on tape.

Before sleep I repeat üks kaks kolm

one two three.

Tigu is snail though this will not help me now.

Cat. Freedom. Flower. Hill. Inside my body your language is growing.

Bell is the same as clock.

Map is kaart as in the German Karte and school is like Schule.

In Estonian it is called kool. Bomb is pomm. Jah is yes.

The word for and is ja. Therefore and is close to yes.

It is a philosophy.

Words, if you know more

add to them

        if you know a lot, sister—

No lack of songs!

We left a whole heap of them on the road

a whole sackfull on the heath.

When we start to sing and let the words

run free then no reins can hold us, no reins

no ropes may bind us.

Thin, elegant bands are too weak and a neat book probably means that the binder has concerned himself more with the appearance than with strength.

Reverting to the original thread for the last—

I now say "ma olen õpilane" fluently which is "I am a student" though

no one asks

my borders vanishing and breaking

to make that sound my lips

are now unrounded without changing the position of the tongue

" . . . words are the only clues we have" on page six is a quote from an interview with Susan Howe in *The Birth-mark: Unsettling the Wilderness in American Literary History*.

The poems on pages 19, 103, and 112 are based on Tarmu Magi's translations of Lydia Koidula.

The line on "octobering" found on page 24 is taken from James C. Scott's *Seeing Like a State: How Certain Schemes to Improve the Human Condition Have Failed.*

On page 37, "I'm in a mirrorless room" is taken from a poem by Yi Sang. On the same page, "Everything is suddenly so full of this wind" and "my own distance stood out still more" are lines from a poem by Jaan Kaplinski.

On page 47, "will slowly free themselves" and "between the sea and the land is a line" are phrases from Göran Sonnevi. The line including " . . . we live in all topological dimensions at once" on page 52 is also an adaptation of a line from Sonnevi.

On page 58, " . . . they dream of being free, and, if under God, directly so" is from Benedict Anderson's book on nationalism entitled *Imagined Communities: Reflections on the Origin and Spread of Nationalism*. The phrase "ghostly national imaginings" found on page 67 is also from Anderson.

The image of a "Talking Book" on page 65 is found in African-American slave narratives and explained in Henry Louis Gates Jr.'s *The Signifying Monkey* as a trope that embodies "The paradox of representing, of containing somehow, the oral within the written . . . . " I do not intend to compare the situation of enslaved

African-Americans to Estonians who were, at various points in their history, slaves in their own land; rather, I borrow this figure of speech to help explicate Estonia's emerging literacy in the late 18th and 19th centuries. The question then of how Estonian literature should sound and how Estonians and Estonia should be represented in text is a question shared by other peoples whose literary history involves simultaneous acts of assimilation and liberation. I use the trope here for its beauty and power as an image, and perhaps to take Gates up on his suggestion that "critics of other literatures will find this theory useful as they attempt to account for the configuration of the texts in their traditions." Yet I believe the trope should not be divorced from its African-American origins, hence this note.

Language on page 78 is taken from chapters in a book, the exact title of which I'm not certain, published by the Estonian Repressed Persons Records Bureau.

Some of the language on page 91 is taken from poet Ottniell Jurissaar.

Language on page 125 is from the Estonian runo song "Laulu Palju," or "Heaps of Songs," researched by Veljo Tormis and recorded by the Estonian Philharmonic Chamber Choir. The Estonian runo is a traditional song form similar to a round; it does not, technically, have a beginning or an end.

On page 127 I am revising the line "Borders always vanishing and breaking" from Jaan Kaplinski.

Language throughout on bookbinding and book repair is taken from *The Thames and Hudson Manual of Book Binding* by Arthur W. Johnson.

Some phrases throughout, occasionally in quotes, are from Estonian language-learning texts and travel guides.

Several collages begin with manipulated pages from a novel by Mait Metsanurk entitled *Toho-Oja Anton*, published in 1924, by the Noor-Eesti, or "Young Estonia" publishing house, a press furthering the Young Estonia movement whose motto was, "Let us be Estonians, but let us also become Europeans!" In 1997, I found the book in a tiny used bookstore in Estonia and bought it for its dilapidated condition, discolored pages, and because I guessed that the publication date and various stamps meant that the book had been rescued from a school library; perhaps it had, at one time, been banned. Other collages include pages from the unpublished autobiography of Eduard Magi, as well as a manuscript version of his story by Reeves Magi. Some of the handwritten materials come from two unpublished poems by Liisa Magi. According to translations by Eino Magi, one poem is about the animals of the forest and the other is about a soldier's anguish and cry for peace. Other documents include a letter from Eduard Magi, notes for his sermons, including, on page 40, images based on doctrine from the Book of Revelation. I found this small sheet of images inserted in one of his notebooks, kept there presumably as a teaching tool, and do not know where it was originally published. The image on page 120 is a song he either translated into Estonian or wrote himself. The image of Estonian soldiers on page 75 is from a postcard most likely made before World War II. Such images were popular during Estonia's brief independence, but were later destroyed, as the photographed subjects were considered "anti-Soviet" or "too Estonian." Finally, some collages originate with maps that were either annotated or created from memory by Tarmu Magi.